# A Wayfinder's Wanderings

## A First Collection of Poems

### Allie Middleton

To Mike ~
rembrances & BCBS
April 2022
Allie

Lulu Publishing Services rev. date: 06/01/2020

Dedicated to the unending universal current of love.

*With heartfelt gratitude to all my teachers and their inspirations, especially my beloved Newell.*

# Contents

*Other Findings*

*Wind*

*Queechy Lake*

*Laguna*

*Forest Refuge Retreat*

*Sun*

*Final Reflections*

# Before the Time Stopped

# Guardians at the Gate

The fire burning
burning flames all around
the waters flowing
flowing and covering all the ground

Our earth turning
turning with tempests raging

The winds trumpeting
trumpeting
and
taking the temples down
and

Space waiting
waiting for our timeless
hearts to awaken.

# What do we trust?

The words that come

    that stillness
    presiding over
    the space that opens
    before and after now

In each moment, a beloved gift

    your invocation
    my incantation
    incarnating all the forms that ever were.

Now landing in a gesture

    a turning
    a further turning
    returning this constant initiation
    our dance
    a bow
    a death
    a door.

# Seven Pieces of Advice from Rumi

In generosity and helping others
>be like the river.

In compassion and grace
>be like the sun.

In concealing others' faults
>be like the night.

In anger and fury
>be like the dead.

In modesty and humility
>be like the soil.

In tolerance
>be like the ocean.

Either you appear as you are
>or
>be as you appear.

# Refuge weavers

Guardians of the light

    the heart as healer
    spine as support
    rooted in earth

       together

Breath as intimate touchstone

    welcoming energies within
    and without

The score emerges

    aligning and attuning to
    what is around
    up and down
    inside and out

       together

We sit to stand

    to lie down
    to travel
    through time and space

       together

Rhythms

unraveling the old
unweaving patterns
welcoming the new treasures

together
and
now

Beheld
we release
weaving the world into being

together.

# Early Morning Light-heartedness

(various)

# Law of Seven, or Music of my Spheres

*(with a smile and a bow to Mr Gurdjïeff)*

*Do*
Standing with the planes of existence,
how might I breathe
and be humble & simple?
Smelling, sensing, listening
to life all around me.

Nothing to do, nowhere to go
and yet my bag of narcissistic
necessities
bogs me down still.

Wanton wandering through
the dust balls of old memories
lives lived long ago
and
promises broken.

What then and where shall I turn?
It seems nowhere
just here now....
Alac, alas...

*where is my beloved?*

Well, right here, next to me,
my mother, myself, all along.

*Re*
Bereft, yet fully contained,
wild yet considerate
mean yet lovable
but always empty

these my narcissistic tendencies.

Wait and watch while
I stop seeking and
bury myself in sorrow
mulching myself ready
for the emergent joy
coming like fireflies in the night.

*Mi*
Resting beneath the pine tree
her boughs singing in the wind
strong kaleidoscopic branches
cascading outward from
a strong center

The earth, warm and softly enfolding me
welcoming me
inviting the
inevitable

listen
here
now

*relax - simply Be*

You are not prey anymore
        now you are free
Let the music enter your bones
        your blood cells
        your heart.

*come dance with me*

*Fa*
A silver dollar for your thoughts
Oh no - no you don't!

No taunting
        please!

What

        am I found?

Impossible, no!

We thought we were

        *invisible*

or was it

        *invincible?*

No
      now it's true
it doesn't make sense to make sense anymore

We are all just like fish
      swimming in the sea
      making music for all to hear

*sing now, dance now,*
*love more and just rest now*

*Sol*
I doubt I kvetch,
      I tremble I retch.
What is this awakening place?
      Why me, my dear god
Who are you
      who has chosen
      to lift us up to see again

      *Who are you*

Or is it that you
      ask me to choose myself
      so as to make room for
      thee and me?

*La*
I overflow and I want
again and again for the
    moment of return

Ordinary ecstasy is the best
just like a bee resting in her nest
knowing honey is already there

*Si*
No matter how long
    I wait for whomever you are
I remain faithful
    to your beauteous bounty
no asking
no telling
    the light just keeps pouring forth

*what to do now?*

*Do*
Nothing.

# Dreaming the Future into Being

## Five Archetypal Poems

# Lift

Here now
exhilarated

experiencing an inchoate
yet inspired something

Now is unique and
connected

In gratitude and
wondering if

together we are sharing
integrity

We rest
broadened and new

now
propelling each other
forward.

# Thresholds of Blue Timelessness

*(what you said as we checked out)*

I
Even if I am just an 'emergent'
attempting to articulate

to speak the words

being in your space and
seeing something
is amazing

staying present
to

knowing
we don't have to teach

it's in the allowing

now

I know why

you were listening to me

now

we've got some thread

staying present

to

common threads

opening circles

    of connection
    on the grid

staying present
to

    a bunch of strangers,
    who never met

staying present
to

    endings and beginnings

even as someone said
and another said

    *be invisible*

our power is
    not to be

our choice is

not to be
    visible

staying present

II

    for invisibility to
    become more present

midwifing what we have to offer

    letting go and letting come
    to what wants to happen now

connecting with
    what we have
to share

sourcing from Homer's blue

now
    impressed with a new form
        as if
    physically touched
by hearing
    your song

and wondering

    *will you come again?*

III
I don't know what it is

I feel as if I went to a movie
    and didn't read the review carefully

    all we did was nothing

IV
yet we heard

    *"thank you all for the time"*

# Ultimate Expansion

Emanating from the center
    we hope for peace

We release fear
    stepping toward freedom

Light guides us
    creating more rays of light

We discover the space of
    new beginnings between endings

Enjoying how mystery and stillness open
    a community of passion and love

New perspectives rising

we recognize a new
    space of listening
    more deeply to
    each other
    ourselves

            and the space in between

Here a pathway of
    innocence opens
a new vision

looking again
toward new life
a creation place
initiating a deeper caring

toward ultimate expansion.

# Love's bold container

In service to connections

    love's bold and fluid container
    creates a family of such potential
    landing amidst the portals

    anchoring golden threads
    releasing our warmth
    as hearts listen

Filled with sweet
    morsels of loving kindness

Trust and humor emerge
    and gales of laughter
    broadcast a new appreciation

Order and disorder
    shape a new aliveness

As space for spirit is redeemed.

# Walls down, water in

In gratitude entwined
breath turning
heads
accepting happy
bodies
whatever forthcoming
speaking and
moving the walls of
allowance and difference

*fluctuations are OK*

now is available and accessible as refreshment
meeting steps or escalator as mirror
welcome breath with
universal breath
attention going in and out
sifting all matter
we are explorers inviting
a radical honesty of new forms
water flowing out
we are here now
finally
sitting
    resting in the center.

# Further Wanderings

## (2015)

# Embracing time

As my vertical self spreads wings out
    around my eyes and
bolts implode upon the earth

my heart scatters seeds and sounds with light

I am perplexed and joyous that we can be seen again
    remorse gone

    *hurrah the fire!*

Joy arising as purple hearts shine toward heavens as
    we sink into space time

        rejoicing in earth's embrace

    remembering we belong.

# A new freshness of pace

Memories whirling by
    swirling in space

cleansing all waters
    as we wander by

Turning wheels
    evermore making sense

of music
    prophets forbore

just as sea and sun and earth
    recognize our songs as dreams.

# From Bompa's chair

When I sat in my grandmother's living room
as a young girl on our Sunday visits

something else was happening

    in between

Looking out the window to the wall of the apartment building
across the alley

    I was

mesmerized by the
    ivy covered walls of the
    apartment building across the way

Swaying with the breeze
    the ivy danced

      in between it all

Realizing that

    I was

more interested
in the moving light
on the leaves
covering the walls
across from us

    I sat and stared

There
in the living room
    people were the backdrop

Watching and listening
the shimmering light

    the dancing ivy leaves

the sound from the songs of the birds
        resting and dancing together

    in between

        I was

hidden from sight
singing

    in between

the space of it all

        I was already

such
    a remembrance

        in between
it all.

*(I missed the way my grandpa read his newspapers in that chair -
he had died recently)*

# Holy fire of Dugan's death

The owl appeared and hooted
appearing and welcoming
the mysterious tremendum
as the timber cracked

resounding

A great house
had been built
alone in the forest

Now felled trees all lined up
pressing in against the massive structure
the clerestory of a life disassembling
never known truly
yet now all crashing down

    forever

Now in this new time
having been destroyed
now destroyed again
sensing old songs and
dances of greatness
fading away

victory remains
incomplete and inglorious

Long forgotten
yet surviving

a refrain

        with an echoing persistence

turns the wheel of time

Traveling now

        toward a new dawn

    willy nilly

And swimming out to sea
in the vortex of a large delta

the gentle outflow
emerging as if from an expiring form

    now with loft and lift

floating

    buoyant at last!

Body is the boat
carrying us
toward the horizon
as water and sky share the
elasticity of existence

    ebbing & flowing
    with every breath

    *is it death or is it life?*

The only way to tell is to
find the feeling of the tensile strength

    on the surface
    of the water

Atmosphere weighting
water goes down with
a fiery handprint on the flow
all met with a smile

Ah
    welcoming sound
a slap
or is it a pat
    an awakening
a voice unbidden
    yet ever present
shepherding us home

Now sinking
    allowing
submergence

    *why not surrender?*

Heart flutters
shudders
then unshuttered,
    flys open
with holy flames bursting forth.

# Peace again

I
All coming again
    we have all come again

I am vetted
I am feted
I am wetted and wed

The streams running deep
    have overflown their keep

From 'way before and 'way below
    a new beyond now emerges

in the flow
no fret
no feet
peaceful and deep

II
I have blown apart
    the wind stripping my sails

a weathered vane now
    ripped and waned
    a tide
    never to be seen
    again

yet we have all come again

*no wonder*

Tides go in and out
     causing and cleansing
     all matter of wart and woof

proof we all come again

III
Shifting yet
     now bending with wind

I wait and meditate

hoping to create
     a new chain
     a glistening of rings

gears turning and true
     a new wheel of circumstance
     singing a new reality

'tho rarely seeming
     to chance
     through old encounters

IV
We all must will
     and heave
ever thrusting

     weaving the sea's breath out
so her sands gently
regain their trust

as death's detritus
spins out a sparkly light

she emerges to remind us of love
before and after

V
Now
we have all come again
that once more

our land may be green
to tell us our stories
singing on the wings.

*a new arrival*
*coming*
*again*
*and again*

# Other Findings

## Mill Creek Retreat

# Mystery Song

The path winds
    on my way to the beloved

Portal after portal
    senses arching
    seeking the way forward
    toward divine song

A voiceless past
    a faceless future
    bubbling sounds that
    ting & ping

Toning shapes that spark
    fires of first remembrance

Mountain paths today bearing
    roots and rocks as
    water meets earth
    singing out
    textures of delight

Feet carries soul forth
    with a desire of heart
    to be found there again

A remaining glance
    toward a still moment
    then plucked out

As secrets after secrets
        release a waterfall
            visited
            so long ago

Life rebounds
        and a mystery song
            reveals herself

Worshiping the aeon
        even as we
            all go on

Unlocking each other and
            sharing newfound keys.

# Ecstasy

My body engaged

I dance and sing

Quietly
ecstatically
excavating the memory
of divine spark

This energetic solution
        of returning
again and again
        since the beginning of time
is heaven

Breaking apart now and
     again from the momentum of time
we are the knowing
     a middle way

We melt into the
        vastness
        renewing each other's endings
        and returning to the
           eternal warm embrace.

# Earth-en Earth-In.

My Mother My Tree
    who sings to me
right here
    at my side

Demanding
    then asking
why aren't you finished with me?

Release me
    love me and let me be

Then dream
    your world
    into being

Oh, hah, hoot hoot
    dear Ma, who are you calling?

    Not Me

    who *is thee?*

    go now
    it's she who I am not

    *who is me?*

'Tho she is still

    here now
    and it is I
    who am not

Yet still

 repeating and releasing
 again and again

Like a dog with a bone
 I learn
 that my song
 myself
 waits deep within
 sacred like every tree

Rooted and in leaf
 or rotten and dying

 *it doesn't matter which*

I am my own tree.

# Raw

If heart is true
    nature
and true nature
    is heart

Where shall I find
    rest
    amidst this
    vast gladness?

We are shorn

Now spinning out a new web
    yet still seared
        by the
    turning and splitting
        of our
    earthly becomings

Might this cutting and shearing
    be the fire
        of
    transformation
    unbidden

    shredding leaves
    and wings
        more naked than
    dead yet

now raw
and fallen?

*solemnly we abide*

Trees say
no space to escape

*remain rooted still*

move toward
this arising
turning earthwards
finally listening.

# In-Between

The old potter at the wheel

    carefully crafting the last vessel
    marked with ancient
    forms and baked true

    radiant colors
    spiraling us between

life and death.

# Here

My head spins
    tapped out
from drinking from
        the roots of paradise

I am
    we are
        in
the garden

Ever and evermore
    snakes
    Adams
    apples
    keep coming

again and again

What we saw
    has been already
    has already been said

What if we surrendered
    to earth's intelligence now?

# Wind

(Maine, summer 2016)

# Going Off Path

Going off path
    I wander
seeking to move
       to re-center

          as my well feels full

Following the energy
so perhaps
        I might empty again.

# Friends, the aimless children

*Part I*

We are all aimless children,
    wandering
like small milkweed puffs
settling sometimes
    on front yards
wafting up porch stairs
    carrying cares from time past

Perhaps a future wishes us forward
    with a freshness of pace

    *now received*

by the eternal breath of inspiration

    and space

As memories whirl by
    swirling in time
space is now
    cleansed by all
sorts of stuff
sweeping off the decks
    of ages passing

Even as I peddle by
    evermore in bliss

pretending
perhaps
to be in stillness

yet making
more sense in-between it all

Continuous tides of change
telling stories of new prophets

witnessing

as sea and earth speak now

*find time again to rest*

*Part II*

It seems we are each chiming in now
rolling like waves
turning shadows into light

Quiet
yet not so quietly present

still evoking

a time past
once regaled

Yet sensing a new presence now

laughing

Mirth and delight
resting
at our own front door

ringing in the bells
of grace and deliverance

*Part III*

We sing our songs
in harmony now

new music abounding

Instruments springing forth
from the unfolding

cascading verses across time and space

Yet inquiry remains
as we emerge and wander
still
circling 'round the mounds of time

Questions arise
asking
is this really it?

When will this really end?

*never ending*

asking whom or what have we served?

*Peace.*

# Queechy Lake

## (October 2016)

# Portals of Potency

i.
The seed bears fruit after a long wait on the vine
dropping morsels of wisdom on the path
beckoning us to follow

Yet now we swim like schools of fish
with all the scales necessary
to release the alchemy of the changing tunes

Yes, it's time for an inner harmony
converging with the new
as the old forms break away

Fogs becoming fugues
new patterns emerging from before and beyond
notes dropping us out of tune with old time

Out of time
lost in time
dancing into new spaces
new shapes

    *yes*

Tasting the portals of potency
trimming and skimming the new reality
    we see

    *time and space dropping away*

ii.
Dead droppings and dyings now
a spine undone

Undulating in space
fluid and spiraling
through all ports of call
we wonder and wander
asking

*what, where?*

"it's not a question anymore of *if* you know how to swim."

The command is great

"Just find your legs and move,
swing your arms too!"

And we spin and spiral
amidst the waves

the light
the wind
the tears

and question our planet again

"where have you been

and

where are you planning to take us now?"

"and for who's sake - what are you needing now
why are you leaving?"

*alas*
*aghast*

*at last*
*we listen*

"stay here
stay rooted
in the ground
earth needs you,

*Reveal Yourselves!"*

Fish swim merrily by
        releasing further scales
solid to our naked eye
        turning and tuning

                the new music
                of time restored

        *eternity emerges*

Music spirals us upward and all around

iii.
Coda

        *what, who, when, where?*

"no one saw this coming"

Submerged now in the becoming
all wet behind the (y)ears
    not knowing

        barely listening
        we hear

Cries of birds
    long informing of this time
    with song

a great potency unfolding
    on the vine

and alas

        falling off
        we listen again
        to the end of old time

the eerie music of icebergs calving
        the frozen hearts and minds

as the ice does its melting

iv
    *Afterwards*

Returning
we learn to swim again
in the mystery of a great new birth

portals opening at every breath

springs gushing forth for healing

singing new songs of truth

New earth forms emerging
        and we walk out of the sea
        to greet each other home
again.

# In these Moon Moments

The sun is illuminating
    the clouds above now
    reflecting in my heart

Ah, sunsets in September...

Water at feet
receives the reflected light
    lapping up beams and spreading
    ripples extending
    kissing the edges of the land

    Earth turns away
now from the sun
awaiting the moon

    Still we sit

in the darkening
in-between
waiting until

now

    And she appears above
bursting into her own

beaming down

*we are here*

now

beaming back and

remembering tomorrow.

# Forces

We tremble with
the force of paradox
on the planet today

We mirror the complexity
in body and mind
our hearts unsure

    once again

and swimming certainly
toward the death of something

The release of
an ancient fire
burning away

    the bitter fruit eaten

seeds sprouted
with
    harvest as hate
as
    anger dances
with
    destruction

    *what more is necessary?*

Halt

    steady stream
denying force

*holy one*
*my beloved*
*turn here*
*knock here*

Let the portals swing open
    angels singing aloft
        hearts opening wide

    once again

reversing this mean rhythm
    and
        opening wide enough

so the belly of the beast
thrashes out its last poisonous timbre

writhing perhaps with
the holy fire of

    our return
    our rebirth
    humanity righted and true

    once again

This wheel of circumstance
    knowing the sorrows and joys
    keeps us turning

We remain on the path
    seeking truth and peace

    once again, turning

    breathing

    and bowing.

# Love in the dark matter
# - songs to silence

Mending and tending tears in the tapestry
our existence breaking apart

connecting earth to body again
sharing ecstasy

Colors and energies
uniting in solid bands
ribbons streaming
screaming

     *"joy!"*

Bodies' riotous
confluences
flowing
through all the waterways

Sill flowing
even weighted

the ever burning embers
    of transformation
greeting each other as one

Spacious elements all around
    air bound and earthbound
    fire and space bound

all at once
　　simultaneously singing

　　*hallelujah*

Listening and singing together again
　　new holy ones
　　　emerge in peaceful union.

# Laguna

(November 2016)

# Hopeful

Waiting and remembering peace
we walk the hills with Venus

I
Each starry night
beckoning us away

Back home now
returned to earth
we remain afloat

Steady chariot
ready now
take me to
my rest

Happy waters
pouring forth
still teaming with toxins
yet complete
     with stories of yore
     spinning
     cascading out
     old
     cycles of
     distress and damage

Oh sun

*where dost thee shine thy light now?*

All our directions
on alert
tilting again
careening
toward some sort of Armageddon?

Speak now
remain fixed
and true

Heart breaking open
again releasing
bones and shards
uprooting old masks

Falsity now
overcome with shame
old costumes
ripping off

*finishing something*

and then

We find ourselves standing together
    spanning the rivers
    awakening intentions
    restoring freedom
    remembering movement
    reflecting light

II
Here now
under the sacred trees
our waters and land sing forth again

Beckoning us to save our precious motherland
        the garden of us all

Linking our branches
bowing with solar energies

Seeded by the sparks
        from the celestial winds

Kissing each newly rooted
seed that springs forth

Sparks shining us forward
wheeling us into a new zone

III
Turning now
offering homage
listening

Hearing the sounds
trumpets heralding

a glorious
new time
on Earth.

# Still restoring, love trembling

This day after
many thousands protest
sitting here at dawn
looking east

    the bright sun rising
    the full moon waiting to shine again
    and our beloved earth
    spinning, spinning

    *what measure beckons us now?*

Where shall we pour our precious beings?

What wants to release still
    so that the new zone can
    still emerge
    and
    cleanse the old
    away?

    *yes*

    conditions of constraint
    and
    ridicule exist

    *protect our most essential home*

Stay erect with the new proportions
    releasing
    disgrace and disease

We tremble and dance away
all matters of distress

Mirrors of separation
dissolving
inviting
hidden souls
to emerge.

*so*

After the first glance
looking again at each other
and trembling

we say

*I love you.*

# Forest Refuge Retreat

## (December 2016)

# Loving my own heart and the heart of the world

Moving from outer space to inner life
I return to a place of contentment
neither here nor there

I go nowhere
    yet I am everywhere

      as my heart relaxes
      into my body

      the earth fills
      springtime feelings

      seeds sprouting
      ready to grow

      I am glad somehow

      moving along
      this path
      I am renewed

    yet
        there is no me

*So, what is it?*

      I sit and listen again
      to the
        wind in the trees.

# Solstice

Methinks the light has returned

*yes*

it's solstice day

I am glad

emerging again

from caves of darkness

we dance again

laying and listening

as the frozen Earth

still cries for us

and the stars

still twinkle

loving us

into existence

stars shining

shimmering

sanctuary glowing with

ancient stories from

plants and planets

all star systems saying

do not abandon us

you are our seeds.

# Light

This light in me, this 'no self'
the empty cabinet of me

I sit and watch and wonder

*how is this all to be?*

Weary traveler of so many ways
I seek to rest and pray

devoting heart
mind and body
speech and song
for love to blossom
to be free

I gave before
I give again
and now ask again

*who are we to be?*

After the great wobble
the light has changed us

Truth has been told

We are not begotten
yet perhaps still besotted
by our own want
and wildness

Our dances diffused
    like an old bad dream
streaming, steaming into
     infinity

We need a new piper who can
    sing magic alive

Again
    behold!

      *we see*

# Fences, you say?

*yes*

we have more straying cows now

Little did I know
    I'm a fence jumping cow

"Independent cow," she said.
    "Yes, and proud now"

*I smile*

How now
spotted stripes and speckled
utterly a new cow
    now
frisky and free

*free I say*

Albeit with chain stains
and marked ears
yet no longer food for
former misery
nor bait for
that fake gate

*at last*

Released now
    in I come
out I go.

# Awakening heart

Is it true you can live and love just from one side of your heart?
 you know, kind of like the way the saying goes
'he speaks from one side of his mouth'

Come on now
 conviction and direction
 take straight-on energy
 not some half-sung song
 without all the parts

Things are moving
 it's coming

The tune just hasn't really
 fully been revealed yet

  *stay with it*

# Potential space emerging

I
Reaching into hidden pockets
        we seek and wander
sometimes going out
sometimes going in
facing and embracing
how to know
this new reality

We freeze and spiral
mesmerized by patterns
     and darkening shadows

making intimidating mountains to climb
        scattering footsteps
        through dark forests
        mind space
        treading through
        swampy torrid waters

Still we seek and seek
     falling all asunder
     until
     the mirage shatters

No earth here

        amidst seduction
        demons of disgrace and despair
        again and again
        released from dances

of failing gravity and
fancy dragons

we see those who do not belong to us anymore

Spirited away
realizing again
and again

as such

as thus

       this the magic
       potential space emerging
       amidst the dross of
       despair disappearing

We share a new view now
       something possible in this
       a beautiful
       emerging reality
       not yet clear

       *try to see from the heart*

What are we seeing and being?
       in the unknowing
       certainly not confined to the
       carousel of time

Now we hear a distance beckoning
a calling for a reckoning

*unstuck*

II
In the distant space
    we dismount the beast of momentum
    and crazy humans' doings

time to breathe
stand still
root now

Savor the threads of peaceful morsels of time
    rethreading
    resounding
    returning
    renewing this
    time of eternity

Spinning and dreaming
    in hope again.

# Being

As time passes
my mind turns to other things.

    somehow
    somewhere
    I have forgotten
    something again

"Who knows?" cackles the crow

    I go out the door
    just another moment of
    wonderment
    remembrance on the path.

# Befriending the fern

I know not why
I know not how
I have become mesmerized
by the fern
in the walking room

Totally taken in by
her majestic wings,
the span of her heart

I stand still in
reverence to
her silent swing
moving and
hearing songs of
beauty and lightness

I rest in her embrace
the swath of sun shining
through her delicate fronds
gently shaping the
shimmering potency of
times to come

Though still
shrouded in doubt
I move closer as she
folds her form into mine
and I rest.

# Sun

## (summer 2017)

# Urging a new arrival

The steamy echo of rain having fallen
    now dampening the trees

    earth's grasses glisten

I sit and smell the afternoon
    my heart weighted with
    the impact
    of time's passing
    and
    the great change

I look again
    to see
    the way the wind lifts
    the ancient songs
    from the leaves.

# Lobster boats wandering at Lincolnville

I

We sat at the water's edge together
cracking open the red carapaces
    drawn up from the ocean floor

      eating

No longer hidden
    precious cargo from future ages past
    we savor each sweet morsel
    admiring the view from where we sit
    watching the ferry boats
    leaving the dock for Isleboro

      eating, eating

We watch
    now seeing
    lobster boats
    nosing into the wind
    as water beneath
    shifts direction

    boats turning, turning
    now pointing here
    now pointing there

    *hum*

whisper the waves
gently lapping the hulls

What are we composting now
  as we enter the days
  they foretold
  stretching
  grasping
  to devour the ages of yore
  yet readying and steadying
  our compasses

  to welcome the new

    *it is truly upon us now*

II
Embarking

I am reminded
  how the horses would stand
  in frozen winter fields
  heads and bodies aligned to the
  oncoming wind and weather

Now the waves ripple
        inviting us to move with it all

Further along the path
        birds line up together
        on the electric wire
        beckoning us listen
        to a future song

Even now
        watching
        seagulls shimmer in solidarity
        feathers aligned by the ocean breeze
        silently welcoming all kinds
        all songs

III
So now
        how might we too
        as humans
        find new dances and songs to rejoice
        reflecting the music of the
        glistening spheres?

        *rest in the silence in-between*

IV
Relaxing into the unending bliss of
elemental connection
witnessing the upending
and our resident becoming

*it's just this*

Together landed in space
welcoming 'the new'

*and whatever is next.*

# Final Reflections

## (May 2018)

# Full moon

I can't stand the stories anymore
it's done, we did it

    it's finished

        *what then, light of the full moon?*

Even as I swim in the lake waters tonight
    I relinquish
    any sorrow

    that's it
    it's over

Yet I'm ready to begin again
    as space reveals herself
    again
    now upside down
    shaping a way into the new.

# No more flames

Inanna the Sumerian goddess beckons us
    bequeathing her
    seaweed crown
    to our eternal
    ghosts

Diving deep now
    never to swim up again
    may the moon gate today
    spread her net wide

Shining even so wide for Indra
    to see and match
    the bejeweled starry
    sounding
    of endings
    in her sky majesty

As waves crash down
    upon our weary heads
    our steeds releasing
    each and every moment
    each brush stroke thus spoke

The new space created now opening in hearts and souls
    so that heaven and earth might
    kiss our feet once more

Adieu, old friend
    go silently now
    go now
    slipping and singing
    swimming down into
    eternal
    peace once
    more.

# Passing Through

Not knowing the way
yet fearing not
I sway

Wobbling between and
    betwixt I say
    shall we move and dance
    playing with sun and moon?

Or sit in trance with stillness askance?

       *the gate appears and disappears*

    each note
    each taste
    each savory
    sensation
    pulling and pushing us
    into the emerging dream

*No more words?*
*No more forms?*

    bowing
    amidst the thunder

    we shall
    tell the story
    of the space
    between the directions
    while

running and walking
standing
sitting and lying down

The sun steals the night
the ice feeds the stream
and a thunderous roar opens

as the holy flame

keeps us silent

passing through the gate

at dawn.

# Times of extraction

Dishes left
other places beckoning
I sit to ponder our work

    in these times of distraction

My heart full
my brain electrified
minds saying yes and no
to the next charge

    oh, these times of extinction

Wanting
taking
pulling
grasping
we careen toward
a
well-known ending

    twisting
    turning
    with fires burning
    winds swirling
    waters filled with
    mud and gore
    creating a new day

Finding times for our awakening once more

    *yes, listen!*

The deeper waters rise
to mind their keep

    ever attending
    ever mending
    as
    space opens
    for

*the new songs.*

# Making Peace Time

Listening to the sound of the bejeweled bullfrog
singing after the rain
I weep

Spring buds
blowing their gentle colors afar
captured by the breezes

> settling into the stream
> singing with stones and stars

making space for
peace time
asking

> *are we perhaps seeing clearly once again?*